Onome Adeyemo

GET YOUR SPARK BACK-

A 30 day practical guide to reigniting the passion in your marriage.

By

Onome Adeyemo

www.sparklingmarriageacademy.com

DISCLAIMER

This book and the items it distributes, contains strategies, methods and other advice that, regardless of my own results and experience, may not produce the same results (or any results) for you. Onome Carolyna Adeyemo makes absolutely no guarantee, expressed or implied, that by following the advice or content available from this book or provided by Onome Carolyna Adeyemo, you will revive a dead marriage, win over an estranged spouse or change your partner's disposition, as there are several factors and variables that come into play regarding any given marital union. Primarily, results will depend on your mind-set, present state of your marriage, your environment, you and your spouse's experiences/backgrounds and other situations or elements that may be beyond your natural control.

URGENT PLEA!

Thank you for purchasing this book.

I would really love to get your feedback and to know how it has impacted your life.

This will definitely help me to make the next version better.

Kindly leave a helpful review on Amazon to let me know your thoughts about this book!

Many thanks. I really appreciate your time and effort.

Onome Carolyna Adeyemo

Onome Adeyemo

DEDICATION

I dedicate this book to every married couple whose once happy marriage now seems bland. May the joyful songs on your lips, the glint in your eyes, the spring in your steps and the fire in your hearts come alive again.

Onome Adeyemo

 Acknowledgement

I express my very great appreciation to God, for strength and life.

I also offer my special thanks to Catherine Egwali, for all the sleepless nights to make this a possibility. To the Oruerios and the Adeyemos, thank you for the immense support.

To all other family members, I say a big thank-you to you all.

To my amazing coach, Temi Ashabi Ajibewa (The Millionaire Housewife), for pulling me out of my shell.

To my friends, you know yourselves… I love you all.

I cannot forget my TSMA family members; you guys are just awesome.

To our lovely jewels, I say a big thank you for being independent as this gave me some time to myself.

Onome Adeyemo

And my special thanks to my Black Prince (BP), who sacrificed so much to see me fly. I appreciate you so much. And thank you for EVERYTHING.

Onome Adeyemo

Table of Content

Introduction

If I was told that three months into my marriage I would be this irritated with the whole idea of being married, I sure would have doubted it. Barely three months after saying 'I do' to my Black Prince, Niyi, I was already caught in the web of distraction.

Please do not crucify me; a lot of things have happened since that fate-sealing day. Sincerely, I did not see this coming. Not even in my worst nightmares. Who would have thought that my marriage would dwindle this terribly? And quickly?

Truthfully, I still cannot remember how we got here. Things deteriorated so much that we could barely carry on a simple conversation without either of us getting upset or worse, irritated. I'm ashamed to say that most times, that someone was me. We drifted apart really quickly and I just couldn't see us heading anywhere but in dooms Ville. Our communication dwindled awfully. I won't even bother to tell you what intimacy meant at such a time. Intimacy? It was far-fetched.

Wait a minute! Before I get carried away with my story, does this have a familiar ring – closely or loosely? Are you experiencing some form of tension in your marriage presently?

Well, my turmoil was about seven years ago and it seems like a lifetime now. I imagine you have picked up this book because it is a topic you can relate to and you are making a choice to turn it around.

Now that you have confirmed you want help to remove the constant friction in your home and you desire a transformation, I am glad to tell you that you are going through your one-stop information resource. Don't be surprised that I know how you feel. I have been there and back; I know how frustrating it is.

Ordinarily, marriage should be fun. I mean real fun, especially when you are with someone you love. But the reverse is the case many times. When couples get married, they naturally find a way to develop their own coping mechanisms as the days go by. All these are done just for society to think their marriage is smooth and rosy.

Meanwhile, if I tried to read your mind this minute, I am sure to find that you would be searching for more effective ways to bring back the romance or passion into your marriage. As demanding as this can be, especially if your spouse is not cooperating, I can only assure you that if you put your mind to it, with conscious and continuous efforts, you will see the light shining in your marriage again in no time.

I know you are thinking – it takes two to make this work. But from experience, I can tell you, it takes only one to make a move for the change. Bother less about whether your spouse is on the same page with you on this or not. We can work with you alone as long as you are willing to do the work required. This is a self-help book, with lots of exciting activities. They will keep you yearning to not just turn the pages, but also to start the next phase of the assignments and apply them to your daily life with your promised-half.

Now, if I may ask – on a scale of 1-5; 5 being very ready and 1 being not ready at all,

- How ready are you to start working on reigniting the spark in your marriage?

- Do you really need the love and laughter in your home back?

- Are you sure that you are willing to go through this route?

If your response to each of these questions fall on 4 on the scale, then it's time to rock 'n' roll!

PROLOGUE

Let's talk about the word 'reignite'. What does it really mean?

The Oxford Dictionary explains it as 'Ignite or cause to ignite again'. So, what does it mean to ignite? The Oxford Dictionary describes it as 'To catch fire cause to catch fire' or in for this purpose, 'To arouse or inflame (an emotion or situation)'. So, putting them together, I would describe reignite to mean *to improve on, to bring back, to transform or to refresh something*. Since you are taking this journey, you either want to fire up or bring the spark into your home. Maybe you once had it, but life happened. Fear not, there's hope.

The fact that you are reading this book shows that you are in, at least, one of these categories. You may be -

- Happily married but you know it can be better and yearn to try harder;

- Not so happily married and your marriage needs help;

- Planning to get married and curious as to how to keep the spark in your marriage when that time comes.

As you know, in this frustrating state of having a bland marriage, every other thing suffers too - the children, businesses, our careers and even our health. Being in an unhealthy relationship is bad but being in an unhealthy marriage is a more terrible place to find oneself.

You know the saying that when two elephants fight, the grass suffers? Same thing applies in marriages and everything we hold dear bears the brunt – the family unit, children, health (especially mental health) and more. An unhealthy marriage does not only stop at affecting the husband or wife involved in it, it goes on to affect the society at large because the children who are termed the leaders of tomorrow adopt their values primarily from the home.

Getting help also means there's a high chance you are willing to break the silence and address the issues. This is a huge step in the right direction because one of the major reasons many marriages suffer is lack of communication.

CHAPTER 1

HOW I GOT MY SPARK BACK

I was born into a polygamous home -this is not news I know, especially as I am from the Southern part of Nigeria. Well, as though that wasn't enough, my parents were divorced by the time I turned five. I grew up with my Dad and he was amazing (God bless him). However, growing up was not so much fun for me because I felt that there was nothing to be excited about.

This had a huge impact on my disposition at home and outside – I barely laughed at home, I reserved all my laughing and excitement for when I was outside the house. This may be because of the way my childhood home was structured.

The situation was so bad that on one fateful day my dad heard me laugh at home (I laughed out so loud and hard), and he said in my dialect- ISOKO, *'Oso ote ro nene'* meaning *'It will rain today.'* To my dad, my laughter automatically meant the day would be a good one because I rarely laughed at home. In spite of being born into a polygamous home, I wouldn't say my home was cantankerous and edgy like people perceive the average

19

Nigerian polygamous home to be based on the movies and stories from several quarters. However, I still felt like something was missing.

While growing up, I kept very few friends (I still do). I did not like drama around me, so I tried to keep my circle within my control. I consider myself a tomboy and I have mostly always behaved like a guy. I would put up a tough front only because I didn't want to be taken for granted.

Sadly, I carried on with this attitude after I got married, giving my husband a first-hand experience of it. At the time, I believed marriage didn't work when women took a lot of mess from their husbands and the society. I was not ready to bear all these, so I had to put a hedge around me. I was not totally living; I merely existed with a lot of pain inside as a result of terrible marriages that I was surrounded with. I just wonder why it affected me so much.

As a young single girl, I saw a good number of people around me who were unhappy in their marriages and this irked me in no little way. There was a particular friend who was struggling in her marriage at some point. Her situation was so bad that she was almost losing herself.

On one occasion, I had just spoken with her before going to church for midweek service and as service progressed, thoughts of her predicament would not let

20

me breathe. I couldn't hold back my tears. I wept so much that the lady sitting next to me offered me a handkerchief. She thought I had lost someone.

With these experiences around me, I resolved not to get married. But our all-knowing and amazing creator looked down on me and said that it will not work — *kolewerk*!

Also, being a tomboy and unlike the average girl my age, a more intimate relationship was never really the goal for me. I had a lot of male friends and one of its advantages was that I found it easy to relate with the men folk. Still, I found it hard to date any of them. I felt too close to get in or get deep. I kept the relationships platonic.

I was only bold enough to accept to date a guy when these words struck me deeply: **as you lay your bed so shall you lie on it.** It began to get clearer to me that if you do not leave some things to chance, nature or society, you will live a healthier life, especially when you allow GOD to be the central focus. Those words brought me great relief and counsel.

At this point, I thought I should have a rethink as regards the marriage decision. This was however, not with full conviction. I was still double-minded about it because I still nursed some pain and anger from seeing other people, especially women, go through semi-hell on earth in their marriages.

Onome Adeyemo

I met my husband during National Youth Service. I was attracted to his calm and gentle nature; such a patient soul with other amazing attributes that I lacked, given my tomboy nature. We dated and courted for about forty-two months before we got married. Just a few months into marriage, those thoughts that I battled with as a result of other messed-up marriages began to flood my mind and these are part of what affected the early years of our marriage.

I was unconsciously irritable and every reaction from me was harsh and somewhat conceited. I clearly remember some awful times as a young wife when I did not see anything wrong with my 'annoying' attitude. I always got on the defensive whenever my husband pointed out my wrong. There were times that while my husband was still talking, I would readily have answers waiting. With this attitude, naturally, I became presumptuous; at times when I was expected to inquire, I failed to ask the right questions. Instead, I would just be acting *Telemundo* in my head. Truly, most times, it is not the unpleasant situation on ground that makes us bitter but the haphazardness going on in our heads.

I almost ruined myself and my marriage but for the gentle soul I have been blessed with. Looking back now, I truly appreciate that place for growth, most especially, for intentional growth. I got to understand that nothing happens by chance, you have to be committed to seeing it through. I was willing to let go of the defensive habit and together, we worked on it. I couldn't have done it alone; I wouldn't have been able to pull through without God's help and of course, my *Black Prince's*.

But is it not incredible how our little attitudes can either destroy or mend us? Bear in mind that these traits will not leave us until we let go. And even when we let go, we must replace them with positive ones. This simply means that if you are letting go of a bad habit like nagging, you must intentionally replace it with an admirable one like regular praise for your partner. This is higher likelihood that this might be achievable if you are ready to put in the work. My mantra on putting problems to rest is: A problem identified is 30% solved, a problem shared is another 30% solved, readiness to put in the necessary efforts yields 20% and taking action leads to a 100% solution.

The turn-around in my life took place three or four years into our marriage, when I was ready to put in the work and steer the change I needed to see in my home. I will highlight below some of the steps I took during this period. I am sure you can find some meaning in it.

Firstly, I ran to God for help because I saw myself pulling down my home with my hands. The Holy Spirit was my first port of call and I had to seek His face at all times. I knew I needed help and only He could save me. It was somewhat easy because I had already identified the problem – me! Hey hey hey, hold it right there, this is not to say I am the black sheep and my hubby is an angel o. Anyway, I knew I was the one who needed help in that regards and I took steps to help myself. I also took to identifying the specific challenges while I worked on positively transforming me.

Secondly, I had not heard about vision-boarding at the time but I understood the power of penning down the things I wished to see happen in my life and I did. I consciously visualized and wrote down the attributes of my dream home. This is because I know that I may not be able to feature in a future I do not picture. This was one of my driving forces.

Thirdly, I had to learn to work it out and stretch myself. I learned from the story of a mother who advised her daughter to always put water in her mouth whenever she was tempted to express feelings of anger, bitterness and unhappiness. This took sheer discipline and determination. I also taught myself patience by thinking through my words before saying them.

Was it hard? Oh, yes! It was like torture and at some point, I felt I was pretending and that the actions I was taking were not the real me. I felt that the real me would explode eventually, when the pressure built up. Neither was it easy to master the art of being silent or editing my thoughts. However, with my husband's patience and my deliberate efforts, not to mention new will, it became easier as the days progressed.

24

Instead of expressing my views while I was still hurting, I learned to stay quiet and only say how I felt after the tension had dissipated. This helped me reduce the number of 'I am sorry' that I had to say. Over time, I argued less and stopped presenting my case in a brash manner. That way, both of us remained calm enough to figure out a solution to whatever problem was at hand.

Finally, I embraced an effective communication system. It requires more than one person to make communication work but it takes only one person to make this change. I told my *Black Prince* to help if he noticed me slipping back to the old me and this did it for me. Even though he hardly came out straight to tell me I was reverting or slipping to the old Onome, he invented other subtle ways of passing this across. Sometimes, it was a simple side-look that told me, *'Girl, you are derailing again.'*

In summary, when you clear your thought path, solutions will come to you. Naturally, you will have a clear head to think things through.

So step back from the scene, look into matters objectively and make the right decisions, especially as it relates to your marriage.

In all these, it was not a smooth ride but gradually, I got better and it reflected positively in my marriage.

I am also thankful for all the Godly people surrounding me otherwise, my life would have become a mess. My *Black Prince,* as I have said earlier, truly helped a great deal because his calm nature alone can quench a raging storm. He introduced weekend outings, once in a while weekday dates and getaways (from the kids). He assisted with house chores and supported me in every way possible. For him, the whole idea is just to help us get closer and reduce the stress, tension and friction that naturally comes with relationships.

Now that you have caught long glimpses of my marriage, let's talk about you and your marriage.

CHAPTER 2

WHERE DID THE SPARK GO?

Nowhere precisely! The spark was subtly chased away by you and your spouse. #BringBackOurSpark

What brought you to the state that you are in now?

For you to be looking to bring back the spark in your marriage, it means that you once had it going well with you. You were once passionate about each other but you both allowed life to happen to you. Do not flog yourself too hard. Look on the bright side: you are alive and in a sane state. As long as you are alive, there is hope.

Let me remind you of some things. This will require you to take time out to reflect on the early days of your marriage. Oh yeah, those 'butterfly-in-your-stomach' days.

Do you remember how you tried to call your fiancé or fiancée (now spouse) ten times a day, speaking for long hours without getting tired? Remember how you would cook a storm and then have trails of perfume at the doorway knowing your bobo or babe was visiting? Remember also how you smiled and bit your lips every

27

Onome Adeyemo

time you hung up the phone or he kissed you goodnight at your doorway? Remember how you couldn't make two sentences without his/her name? Yes, you remember all that but what happened? Routines, kids and the business of life have slowly robbed you of those butterfly moments, haven't they?

Have you thought hard about why and how things got this bad?

Have you and/or your spouse taken out time to analyse the dwindling state of your relationship?

Do you and your spouse still communicate actively? Or are both of you just placid?

Remember, that being placid is a terrible state to be and remain in. No matter what it is, you must make conscious efforts to see that your relationship with your spouse blossoms unless both of you have agreed to go separate ways. But why would you?

It is a lot easier to bring back the groove into your marriage if both parties are ready to make it work, but if you are alone in your desire for improvement, do not despair.

To set this off on the right course, you will be required to have a long and crucial talk with your spouse (probably after reading this book together) to find better ways to make your marriage blossom again. Cheer up, there is hope.

28

Here are a few questions to ask yourselves:

A. How long have you been married?

B. What could have gone wrong?

C. When did the changes start?

D. Where is the spark that both of you experienced in your early years together?

E. How did things get this bad?

F. What would you have done differently?

G. Do you have kids yet? Could it be the presence or absence of kids that is causing the change?

H. Is either or both of you financially stressed?

I. Could it be any of the following?

- Over familiarity?

- Lack of communication?

- Lack of creativity?

- Distractions (social media, gadgets, in-laws, family members, children or friends)?

- Comparison?

Let's look at some of these points in greater detail.

A. Over-Familiarity: In my first two years of marriage, I remember that whenever my husband told me that he would be away for two days, I would almost fall sick because I did not want to be far from him. I wanted to be with him as long as we were not at our different places of work. However, as time went on, I realized I began to get used to him being away for one week at a time. It got to a point that I began to look forward to him travelling because I felt I needed my space.

Yes, everybody at one time or the other, needs an alone time or me-time but I'm depicting a different scenario here. The spark partners feel at the beginning of their marriage may fly away without both parties noticing it quickly enough. This is more because of over-familiarity. If you let it, it breeds contempt and is the beginning of loss of respect.

Carry out a personal analysis; do you feel the same way, or even better, about your spouse as when you just married them? It is simply natural. When two people stay together or relate often, they tend to overstep their boundaries. This is very common in marriages.

What is the solution to this problem? Intentionality. We must be very deliberate not to become too familiar with our spouse or get caught in routines.

B. Lack of Effective Communication: Communication is one of the major pillars in marriage. 'A marriage without effective communication is worse than a Ferrari without an engine'.

One of my clients, Nkem, complained that their relationship turned sour just after a few years of married life. After discussing with her a few times, we discovered that she and David (her husband) had gotten to a point in their marriage where all they talked about were basic and direct topics such as housekeeping and their children. A typical conversation was, "I need money for school fees or money for home management." and the money would be provided. There were no deep or personal conversations. There were no discussions that helped them bare their hearts or even let down their guards. What they did not understand was that, this lack of deep or intentional communication had made everything in their marriage sour.

As an intentional partner, listen consciously with an open mind and not with a preconceived idea, so as to prevent bigoted views or opinions. Listening with a preconceived idea usually distorts the flow of information and makes you respond without actually getting what is being said.

When you are bent on defending yourself always, you will totally misunderstand what your spouse is saying. When you apply the defence mechanism, you might unintentionally stir an attack or worse, total silence from your spouse.

This might inadvertently destroy your communication with each other. As we know, a marriage with no communication is dead already.

To improve on this, one needs to

- master the art of listening,

- kill the temptation to respond to every sentence made by your spouse,

- at least allow the other party to finish talking before you err your opinion.

- as much as possible, erase every preconceived idea about the subject matter so as to allow you think with a clear head and give objective responses.

- do aware with assumptions, it kills faster than aids

- ensure not to conceal information, ask questions to gain clarity, err your views politely so that both parties can easily relate better.

C. Lack of Creativity: As we progress in marriage, we notice that we begin to unconsciously display some level of nonchalance. Be ready to become everything to your spouse, being able to play different roles at different times to him/her. Do the Unusual/Get Creative, do not remain stuck in your routine; change is the only constant thing. If you have been doing something

Onome Adeyemo

the same way for six years and you have been getting unpleasant results, it's high time we looked elsewhere and did things differently. What do you think?

To make our marriages more fun, we need to embrace:

i.   **Creativity in your looks:** Physical appearances prove there is more to looking good than vanity; change your looks from time to time. As a female, apply mild make up at home; it might just be lip gloss or lipstick so that he will not be able to predict you. Be clean, fresh and presentable at all times so that when your spouse asks you to meet them somewhere, they will not be scared that you might wear something that will cause them shame. Dress in a way that your spouse will look forward to showing you off to his/her friends.

ii.   **Culinary creativity**: Prepare your spouses' favourite meals at least twice in a month, learn other types of food and ask for improvement ideas. Be bold, check out food blog sites, recipe pages, watch food channels and even YouTube.

iii.   **Sensual creativity**: learn to pull stunts in bed and especially for us women, this cannot be over-emphasized. It is not an assurance that your husband will stick to you for life and as a man, the fact that you do your homework well does not mean that your wife cannot cheat on you. It just helps to bring some sort of newness into your home.

Do *IT* differently, do the heard and unheard of and do not be stuck with the same old same old tricks.

If you think the passion in your marriage is cooling, you need to heat it up. Whether or not your spouse is willing to roll with you, just play your part. Initiate some fun and new ways to do the regular things you would ordinarily do. You need to leave your comfort zone if you really yearn to see and enjoy newness in your marriage.

iv. Buying of surprise gifts: Give your spouse gifts *just because*; they don't have to be expensive and you need not wait until there is an occasion (birthday or anniversary).

v. Get Playful: You could add sticky notes with nice words at strategic places such that the first note directs your partner to the next and so on.

Generally speaking, we can improve on our marriage more if only we consciously do many of this basic things we have ignored.

- Do something new together every week.
- Say the words, I love you, and mean it.
- Be ready to learn and improve yourself on the different areas of your life.

34

D.   Unhealthy Interferences

When people encounter you, what perceptions do they have of you and your attitude towards your spouse or marriage? Do you give them the perception that your marriage is a priority to you? Trust me, people get these vibes.

Do they see you as one that value your marriage more than external relationships or is the reverse the case? Here are some interferences that are likely present in your marriage and ways to deal with them.

    i.   **Gadgets and Social media** (Phones, Tablets, Twitter, WhatsApp etc.) **:** To deal with these distractions, simply

* Turn off notifications while you are together,

* Exit groups that adds little or no value to you (Facebook groups, WhatsApp groups, etc.),

* Engage in gadget-free outings and sometimes you could embrace gadget time-out (doing away with your phone). This can be indoors so that you can bond more,

* Take permission from your spouse when you want to do important tasks on any electronic gadget to avoid making them feel ignored. Taking permission does not mean you are enslaving yourself it only shows that you respect and value your relationship with your spouse more.

* Reduce the workload you bring home from your business or work.

35

ii. **Family:** How well do you think your family have added to you? Are the people around you helping you enjoy marriage better or are they draining you? Dealing with family is a bit dicey because you may not be able to cut off from family as easily as you would have done friends.

- For family, you can create a little distance by reducing the number of times you reach out to them. Remember, this is if the family member falls within the category of people that needs to be cut off.

- When you are around them, limit the questions you ask so that the conversation will not linger longer than you need it to.

- Finally, stop laughing too hard or giving gestures that portray that you are enjoying the conversation which automatically means that you are around for a while. Oh yes, smile but do not laugh out too loudly.

iii. **Friends:** To start with, you need to do some tasks.

- Create a mental list of your friends and how well they have made your life better.

- Keep only few intimate friends (maybe two or three); the fewer the better.
- Keep only friends who have respect for your spouse and who give value-adding advice.
- Carry out a life audit from time to time as you are not glued to anybody, not even your twin. Remove the people who do not add positively to you and guard jealously the ones that make you better and not bitter.

There are some people that just want to suck and drain life out of you. Most times they only say and see negativities around you, just let them go. Remember that your placenta is not glued to theirs.

E. Comparison: This is a thief of time, a killer and a disease. It rids one of peace and joy. Comparison kills marriages faster than HIV.

Do not ever be caught in the web of comparing yourself or your spouse with someone else. Remember that whenever you compare, you are comparing the other person's outward strength or results to your inner weakness or efforts.

I know that at this point, you are probably recalling incidences when you did not practise these tips. You are also worried that it may be too

37

late to begin to steer your marriage around. Relax. Just take a deep breath. Do not over flog yourself.
Marriage may be hard work but it can really be fun if both of you put in the work together.

Let me digress a little, how true is this? I once read that a couple's sex life at the beginning of a relationship becomes different during a long-term relationship. The former is usually described as intense, exciting and frequent while the latter feels more comfortable, is often predictable and likely not to happen twice a day or everyday like it used to.

So, if I may ask, how do you feel about love making? Is it still as amazing as it used to be when you just got married? How have things changed?

Think about your honeymoon days...they were awesome, right? Do you know that love making with someone you have been with for years can still be as exhilarating as it was the first times you slept together?

While bringing back the spark to your home is not necessarily about making love, it is an important part of it although, it is only a fraction.

You must make every effort not to fall into the group of people who use the presence of children or financial constraints as excuses for sexual problems. These problems are not insurmountable or peculiar to you alone. If both of you really want to make it work, you will find a way; if not, you will find an excuse.

So, let's dive straight in.

What are those simple actions you can take to bring back the excitement, intimacy and affection you felt when you just met?

Remember that movie, How Stella Got Her Groove Back?

Yes, let's get the groove back right away.

CHAPTER 3

READY TO GET YOUR GROOVE ON?

MUST DOS

There are some basic things that must be carried out or followed through when you are deliberating about reigniting the fire in your marriage. They include:

1. **MIND WORK:** Everything begins and ends with the mind. You must be open to learning, unlearning and relearning. You must be a life-long student who is open to positive change and growth.

Why am I focused on mind work? Picking up this book and getting to this point will only mean one thing – there is an 80% or 90% chance that you are ready to do what it takes to reignite the passion between you and your spouse or if you are not married yet, you are looking at possible ways to reignite the spark if it begins to fade at some point. Trust me, chances are that it will happen; it's a phase.

Firstly, it must start with you. It begins with a decision and a renewed mind-set. To get back on track, you need to work on the inner chambers of your mind to dig deep

41

Onome Adeyemo

and search for the possibility that the spark can return to your home no matter how bad it seems. Stay optimistic even if you are in doubt based on some unpleasant events from the past. Conquer the battle in your mind; I believe in you, you can make it work.

Remember that what you focus on, you become. Dwell on the positives because if you think it will work, it will; if you think it won't work, it will surely not. To this end, you must develop a growth mind-set and not a fixed mind-set.

Are you ready to go on with this sparkle gist or is it becoming a little scarier?

You need to purge your mind and thoughts in and out. Consciously, look inwards and then outwards. As you read, what is going on inside of you? What have you focused on — the negatives? Remember that what you focus on expands.

Ask yourself how your past has been- good, bad or ugly? If it has not been pleasant, be sure to purge your mind. This exercise heals us of any past pain we have experienced such that when you hear the name of the person who hurt you years ago, you will just smile, shrug your shoulders and move on without nursing any pain or guilt. Conquer the battle of the man inside first and the one outside will be defeated.

Feed your mind with positive things. Positive thinking breeds positive outcome. In simple terms, Garbage in Garbage out (GIGO).

Here are the steps for you to take while doing the mind work:

- Cleanse your head from ills;
- Forgive yourself and any other person that may have caused you pain;
- Learn to trust again, live your life and be yourself;
- Engage in mind-purge from time to time;
- Embrace the use of daily confessions and affirmations.

Romans 12:2 puts it so accurately, *"And be not conformed to this world; but be ye transformed by the renewing of your mind."* Change only comes easily when you have caused your inner man to align with your desired goal.

Proverbs 4:23 reads these important words, *Guard your heart with all diligence, for out of it flows the issues of life.* This verse somewhat implies that a negative mind will never give you a positive life. Remember, your mind is your garden while your thoughts are the seeds so you will either grow weeds or flowers.

In trying to get our minds attuned right, one of the solutions will be complete cleansing; that is, letting go of hurt and pains. Some of the suggestions I have put down below can be helpful in handling hurtful situations.

43

How to Handle Hurtful Situations

- Accept the situation. While it may be difficult, you must accept the reality that the pain-inducing experience happened. Stop living in denial.

- Let it go first from inside and then outside because you cannot win on the outside without first winning on the inside.

- Free your head. Be at peace with yourself. Forgive yourself and every other person who has hurt you.

- Take a bold step further by openly expressing your feelings so that you can get closure.

- Move on for good.

2. **INTENTIONALITY**:

This is my mantra - *I am ready to make my marriage a lot better by becoming more deliberate in my dealings.*

- Are you joining me in this campaign?
- Are you ready to become more deliberate?
- Are you willing to balance your work and other areas of life so that no specific aspect suffers?

The truth about enjoying life and having a blissful marriage is that you have to be ready to let go and sacrifice some pleasures just to satisfy your spouse and/or children. This, of course, you should do happily and not grudgingly.

Becoming more intentional also solves the problem of over familiarity. If at least one partner deliberately or consciously does the things that he or she knows will bring the union back to its original happy state, then life will be a lot better for us all.

I remember a period I noticed that the time spent on my laptop and phone increasingly began to interfere with my relationship with my husband. However, the mere fact that I had decided to become intentional about my moves made the decision to let go of my gadgets easier, not completely of course, but to a reasonable minimum. There is the need to balance things always, so that other aspects of our lives will not suffer.

3.   GENUINE FORGIVENESS:
This can be very difficult sometimes, especially if the weight of the pain caused is really deep. Although in the long run, forgiving your spouse or anyone even does you a lot more good than you can imagine.

This helps you move on faster and further than you can think of. People will naturally hurt us, I say this often. If your wife grew up in Cameroun and you were groomed in Kebbi state, what makes you think that you will not have issues or face challenges? Even twin siblings fight sometimes, how much more you and your spouse who most probably have very diverse social upbringing. So, when trying times come, do not see it as the end, it is just another curve in the road of *spousal learning*. Ensure to be by your spouse especially when you know that he or she genuinely needs you. Love your spouse through God's eyes.

Avoid referring to issues of the past. Let go and let go completely; erase the residues. Forgive easily because holding grudge destroys marriages fast. An unforgiving attitude causes heartache; it makes you feel choked and is dangerous to your health. Even the doctors, no matter how good they are at their jobs, may see nothing wrong with you except if they ask very personal questions. If you feel so bitter because of the past events happening in your home and you feel you cannot deal with it anymore, please seek help and tell GOD your pains. As much as possible learn to forgive always.

Now we are getting closer than you think. In the next chapter, you will be given daily tasks to accomplish. The spark will not just come back because you wish it to. I need not remind you of the saying, ''if wishes were horses......'' You must put in the work; even prayers alone cannot bring it back. So, let's get started already. Are you ready?

Onome Adeyemo

CHAPTER 4

LET'S ROCK THE REAL DEAL

Whoop! Whoop!

Congratulations! You have made it to this chapter.
I believe it takes great effort to bring this spark back hence, we have bent over backwards to support you in the next thirty days. I will love to hear your experience during this challenge and understand how these routines helped bring the spark back in your marriage.

Here begins the thirty-day challenge. The idea behind this is to help you rekindle the spark speedily.

> 1. Firstly, it must start with you - the man in the mirror. It starts with a renewed mind-set. You need to work on your mind to see the possibility that the spark can come back to your home, no matter how bad it seems right now.
> Own the victory in your mind, you can make it work.
> NOTE: If you cannot get past this point (renewing your mind) then nothing you do will matter. Every other energy spent will be wasted.

48

2.   Hug your spouse daily (preferably in the morning) for, at least, fifteen (15) seconds. You might be wondering why fifteen seconds. When you do this and you truly put your heart to it, you will realize that you would have lost count by the time you get to the 8th second. Try this and let me know how you feel afterwards. I'll really love to read from you.

Lest I forget, while at it do not say a word to your spouse.

3.   Kiss your spouse every morning when you wake up and, at least, once before you leave the house. This should continue when both of you return in the evening when both of you have returned home for the day. I know some couples live in different cities but when you are together, you may practise this. Please, improve on your kissing pattern and ditch the same old same old. Try something new; check YouTube for tips.

4.   Forgive yourself and your spouse of any hurts you feel. Preferably, talk about it at an appropriate time and in a non-confrontational manner so you can be free from inside – continuously do a mind purge.

5.   Remember, your spouse is your first baby. When you are in bed and getting ready to sleep,

ensure you cuddle your spouse, this will give him or her, a relaxed heart and smooth sleep.

6.   Make sure you reach out to your spouse (by call or text message) at least once today not to make inquiries or for no specific reason other than to say I love you or I just need to hear your voice. This will help to ease the work stress and brighten their day. Think about it, how will you feel if your spouse calls you during work hours to say I love you?

7.   Sit on your spouse's lap at any given opportunity today, especially as a wife. Lean on each other and hold hands as often as possible no matter where you are.

8.   When you lie down to sleep, make sure you have body contact. Ensure you touch toes as this reminds your spouse that you are there and you still care a lot about them. This works so well especially when you both are having a misunderstanding and you do not know where to start apologising from or trashing the issue on ground.

9.   Be vulnerable. Oh yes, be vulnerable. I know this is very deep. Let yourself out, be open to your spouse and let them see through you like a mirror. But you might want to tread carefully here

50

and be sure that your spouse is also willing to be open. That way, you don't get badly burnt. When couples are vulnerable, it is easy to flow with each other as neither party will feel too exposed.

10. Touch your spouse often. This must not always lead to lovemaking but it should create a strong bond such that when lovemaking finally occurs, you will be in high heavens. At every place, any time you walk past your spouse today, do something. Just touch her bum or rub his chest and back it up with a smile or a wink.

11. Appreciate your spouse today. Yes, no matter how little they have done for you or the home. Even if your spouse only turned on the generator, did the dishes or cared for the kids, ensure you appreciate every effort as a show of kindness. The truth is, when you appreciate your spouse, you get them to do more things for you with ease.

12. Spend at least 10-15 minutes today in trying to bond and connect with your spouse, talk about how your day has been, especially at the end of each day. Share experiences as this helps you feel as though you were a part of your spouse's day.

13. Let your family and friends know that after GOD, your spouse is your **first priority.** They will appreciate that and mind their boundaries. The way you treat your most priced treasures will determine how others will treat them too. Same applies to your spouse; if you put them down, others will (un)consciously mistreat your spouse too.

14. Weekends are for fun, watching movies and going out. Weekdays can be included too, so today, schedule a fun date with your spouse. You can make this a ritual and you will see how closely knit you will both become.

15. Prepare your spouse's favourite meal today or at least, twice a month henceforth.

16. Endeavour to support your spouse with their chores today, a few times in a week and as often as possible. If as a husband you rarely help with house chores and child care, today is a great day to help out. As a wife, be patient with his attempts at helping out and appreciate the efforts. Kindly, do away with those friends that say a man should not help at home and a wife should not be involved in supporting her husband's career/business. If you do not help your spouse, who will?

17. Reduce the number of times you complain about your spouse today and praise more than you criticize. To make this easier, list a number of things you like about your spouse or something they do well and for today at least send them one text every 3 hours appreciating them for each of those traits.

18. For today, consciously take your bath together. Oh yes! make it fun time too. Let this be an activity you both look forward to everyday if it's possible. You can even make it so interesting that when someone defaults in meeting the other in the bathroom for no genuine reason, he or she pays a fine. However, stick to what works for you.

19. Drop sticky notes with kind words in strategic areas around the house, preferably your bedroom. Tell your spouse how much you love and appreciate them in your life. One sticky note can direct them to the next just like we see in treasure hunts. If well done, it can turn out to be such great fun and make both parties play like little children.

20. Be lively and friendly with your spouse today. Always have a cheerful and welcoming look and if you are disturbed about anything, talk about it. A welcoming atmosphere will make your spouse willing to run home to you.

21. Share a sexual fantasy and propose trying it out. Do not fail to tell your spouse to make love to you in a way you like. Even if they do not do it eventually, it would have passed through their thought. Trust me, they will process it and get back to you sooner than you think. Besides, it's not a big deal. Just talk.

22. Develop codes for your bedroom language. For example, I need a trip to JERUSALEM, the last trip we had was real fun. Let others around you keep wondering what *trip to JERUSALEM* is. The kids or other family members should not know what you are referring to. This makes it even more fun.

23. Take a few minutes' walk within your area or around your house today. Consciously make it a routine activity to participate in together from time to time (weekends). Do not allow your kids to be the barrier. If you need help with the kids try to get help from trusted relatives, neighbours or friends.

24. Communicate and honestly express your feelings about sex to each other. It is amazing that some couples do not talk about sex. It's not a sin, please talk about it. Say how you feel when it comes to love making and intimacy. Are you very

satisfied? Is there something you need your spouse to work on?

25. Get your spouse a surprise gift(s) today. No matter how little, it is the thought that matters, not the cost of the gift. There must not be a special occasion or event, just do it.

26. Ask your partner what you can do to make him or her happier. As you ask, be ready to unlearn, learn and relearn. Be open and flexible such that when your partner suggests that you do something new to spice up the marriage, you can easily jump at it.

27. Make love in an unusual place today. Depending on your schedule today, you can drive to a secluded area and have sex in the car or on the beach. If you must be inside your home, clear the coast and take away any form of distractions - the kids, domestic staff, relatives, etc. Take over your home and freely make love in every corner of the house except your bedroom. As much as you can, do not make love at night alone. Do it in the morning, afternoon or evening. Get down in the garage, kitchen, children's room, laundry room, everywhere.

28. Be grateful to your spouse for choosing you. If you have been following this challenge

properly, it will make them feel really loved, appreciated and important. Tell your wife 'thank you' for accepting to be your wife or say thank you for choosing often.

29. Never assume that you know what to do to your spouse that will make him or her a better person. Always ask them, *"What can I do to make you feel loved and appreciated?* Ask! Ask! Ask!

30. Be creative today and let the change come from you. Do those things you have never done to your spouse before. Brother, please play with madam's clitoris and bring her to Cloud Nine. Did you say yuck? Oh, you are missing big time. Try it and see your wife in a different realm of glory. As a wife, have you ever tried to use your hidden talents while playing with your husband's brain box? Please do not ask me what brain box is just check in between his legs…did you say no? Haba! Renew your mind and take it as an assignment today. Do it and come back to testify. Explore, while making love to your spouse, you may introduce the use of honey, chocolate or ice.

31. Finally, ensure to talk to GOD with your spouse today and always. Apart from praying for your spouse, make sure you pray with them today and always. I am super excited because for this task

56

distance is not an excuse. Bear in mind that a family that prays together, not only stay together but slays together. Do not skip your daily devotionals together, especially if you both stay in the same house. Study scriptures together and discuss lessons learned as often as possible.

Hahaha, I am very sure some of these tasks hit you like an impossibility. Not because you cannot get involved in them straight up but simply because you are asking yourself these questions:

- Why should I go to this length?
- Why must I be the one to make these sacrifices?
- Why should I have headache because of this partner of mine that doesn't seem to care? Why, Why, Why?

In any case, I want to believe that you were able to go through these exercises.

DO NOT READ THE NEXT CHAPTER, UNTIL YOU HAVE DONE ALL THAT THERE IS TO BE DONE IN CHAPTERS 3 and 4. IF YOU HAVE NOT DONE THEM, THEN SLIDE BACKWARDS AND COMPLETE THE TASKS.

THE NEXT CHAPTER WILL BE TOTALLY USELESS, IF YOU REFUSE TO PERFORM THE TASKS.

CHAPTER 5

FINALLY, WE MADE IT

Now that you are done, I can boldly say congratulations. You made it!

How does it feel to go through the process of trying to bring your spark back?

I guess you enjoyed the full process and you have most likely made a decision never to allow yourself and your partner return to that terrible state again. Because we cannot assume to know what our spouse's needs are, we must continually;

- Ask questions for clarity. It is known that we can never go wrong by asking the right questions. Memories of when we started out as a couple flood back as I write this. I had this little fear of carrying through with being me. You might be wondering why I had that fear after all, well it was because I know that some people tend to change from who they were while they were dating. Do not allow the fear of being shut down keep you from expressing yourself. As

59

long as *how* you say, *what* you say, *when* and *where* you say it is good enough.

Over time, we (my *Black Prince* and I) have built system of 'talk about anything and everything' no matter how bad it seems. Just be open to talking about it or at least, create an enabling environment where your partner will be free enough to talk about anything with you. Remember you must be trustworthy so that your partner can be vulnerable enough to let out his/her feelings.

Some of these questions will help you create a stronger bond with your spouse, when you ask them the right way. For example:

- What would you like me to do to make our relationship better?
- Am I satisfying you in bed enough?
- Is there any issue/concern you think we need to talk about?
- What makes you come alive?
- What are you passionate about?

All these questions are just to help you start conversations. They will help you know each other more and help to figure out if both of you are enjoying yourselves in the marriage or not.

Onome Adeyemo

Finally, I just want to know.....do you have a family vision? If no, please work on having one. Having a clear joint vision helps to create a stronger bond with your spouse while ensuring that you both stay on the same page page through life. Let me not cause an adrenalin rush to to your brain with so much information as regards reigniting the spark in your home.

But if you got to this page without following through on the exercises, you are probably wondering if these tasks will be helpful at all. Below are a few of the most alluring feedback from our success stories, not that we have any unsuccessful stories. Lol! I implore you to try more than a few, put your own twists to them, start small and explode as you get comfortable with the tasks and events.

Hold on to your book tightly as you read some jaw-dropping, riveting reports which I originally thought should be exclusive (SP&C). Hahaha!

It is my joy to bring you this TMI gist from real TSMA sparkle gems who gave me permission to share their stories. My sincere prayer is that you are able to find a gem in you and more jewels in your marriage to bring the sparkles back to your home.

Onome Adeyemo

"My name is Obiajuru Luya, CEO of Truace Consulting, manufacturer of Kwikmil Foods, and Convener of the support group, GrowHub.

I'm married to my long-time friend who bulldozed his way into my life at a time when I had a long list of suitors. Lol!

Our marriage has been relatively peaceful, not without the usual disagreements and differing opinions, but God has constantly helped us resolve our issues, grow in love and stay happy.

When Onome Adeyemo, the TSMA boss lady started and invited us to the academy, we joined because she is 'our person' and we wanted to support her but I must say that she has made us more lovey-dovey than ever before. Hubby says I am 'naughtier' than before, we share more codes and laughter and I tease him a lot about reporting to his sister, our TSMA coach over every flimsy thing. TSMA has brought even more gist and laughter to my home and marriage.

I've also come to learn that the little things really matter - touch your toes together when you sleep, cuddle without lovemaking, share old pictures, and place your head on his chest.... These things and more have helped us connect better and helped me be more forgiving when he upsets me.

I'm thankful for Onome and I'm thankful for TSMA. I hope that more couples would become more intentional about making their marriages sparkle, not the peripheral kind of make-believe sparkling but a genuine connection that oozes out of a truly happy heart. We've got it and we're keeping it. Join us!"

O. Luya (CEO of Truace Consulting and Kwikmil Foods)

Onome Adeyemo

"I recall being in a position of always receiving and wanting my husband to be more, do more and love more while I was not in the giving zone. I always felt sad that my 2^+yrs of marriage wasn't quite as exciting as I had envisaged.

Then one day, I just needed someone to share my issues with and Onome Adeyemo came to mind. She literally showed me how and where I needed to improve upon which included reducing the hours I spent on the phone and creating some alone time for us.

" can categorically say that things are changing for the better already."
G. Wabara (THE EMPLOYED ENTREPRENEUR)

"I just want to say thank you for the 28-day challenge. I just started mine and it's working very well. Thanks a lot. You are awesome and I really appreciate it. My husband, Boo, started calling me pet names again and he is now more caring than before.

I worked late last night so I didn't wake up early this morning; before I woke up, he had made me breakfast which he hasn't done before. In my mind I was like, "Is this really happening?"

G. Ibigoni (An Enterepreneur)

Onome Adeyemo

"I want to thank Coach Onome Adeyemo especially for this five-day love spice. My husband had been moody since giving birth to our twins. However, yesterday, after reading your I knew I had to do something very creative in my marriage.

On Day 1, immediately he called to say he would be home late, I told him I had a surprise package for him from overseas and urged him to come home a little earlier. He said ok. He came home at about 7pm. My outfit was very smashing, if I may say so myself. I opened the door and gave him a hug and a passionate kiss. Wow! He was speechless. When his response came, he blurted out, "So honey, you are really this romantic?"

On Day 2, he came back early and said, "I can't wait for today's surprise." I asked him to carry one of the twins, which he did without grumbling. This was in preparation for the gift. Meanwhile, sometime ago, I gave him a silver bracelet just after we got married but he lost it when he went to repair his car and he was sad for about two days. I had to go to the mechanic workshop myself today to look for it and I didn't give up till I found it then I gifted it back to him. Coach Onome, he jumped up and down as if he won a lottery. I never knew he cherished it.

Day 3, as he was leaving for work he asked me if there was any surprise that day. I said yes. Then he asked if he should come home on time. Wow! My Coach, I was speechless. I asked myself, "Is this my husband?" So I set a track and trail surprise for him; if he can find me (treasure hunt), he will receive a blow job (lol!) but if he doesn't, he will dance for me. I knew he would come home early so I hastened up in writing and *pasting clues on how to find me. It was fun but he didn't find me and he ended up dancing for me. But it was pure fun and these acts helped to reignite the intimacy between us.*

On Day4, I woke him up with the aroma of his favourite dish; you should have seen him pacing up and down the dining, peeping to know when the food would be ready. We enjoyed the meal together and he was truly happy.

On Day 5, I told him to concentrate at work and that I would be there with him and from the moment he closed the door, I started sending him romantic messages. I never knew my husband was equally romantic as he was responding immediately too. Just before 1pm, he was back home. He saw me struggling to make the twins comfortable and the next thing he said was, "Honey, you can rest; I will take it from here."

I was shell-shocked because he usually doesn't like helping out with the kids but that day, I saw my husband feeding the twins one after the other, changing their diapers and equally singing them to sleep.
Coach Onome, I never knew that the sweetness of marriage depends on how you mould it. In five days, my husband changed positively. See my husband that I have been begging and pleading with to come home early; in five days, I changed the story of my marriage. In five days, I realized who I got married to.
I am the happiest; I can't even thank you enough.
I am glad I partook in this five-day love spice.
God bless you, ma. God bless TSMA."
C. Levi

Onome Adeyemo

"The Sparkling Marriage Academy (TSMA) is the place to be for every couple that needs to change for good, regarding issues that are centred on intimacy and passion for couples. TSMA has really helped to bring sparkles into my marriage but most especially, it has helped to transform my mind-set towards marriage. TSMA has helped me to look beyond my spouse as the one at fault and I now consciously look inward to see the role I am playing in making my marriage experience bitter or better.

The teachings from TSMA have made me realise that we are not perfect and neither are our spouses. This has helped me in managing marital issues better and I thank GOD for the founder of TSMA (Mrs Onome Adeyemo) for taking it upon herself to ensure that marriages truly SPARKLE.

O. Sanyaolu (Founder SARA Clothings – Lagos)

Onome Adeyemo

Conclusion

Well, these and many more testimonies abound in TSMA. I know these few tips will help to rekindle the fire in your marriage and home. Always remember that nothing happens by chance; you must do the needful.

Do not get carried away with activities and get overwhelmed with the events that follow marriage. All these can easily wear one out. Apart from GOD, focus on your partner more than every other person or thing.

Marriage is sometimes seen as hard work but truthfully, the work is not as hard as we think if both parties are ready to do what needs to be done.

As an individual, you must **Be The Change You Wish To See**.

If you need clarity on how to create a family vision or you desire that I assist you in the journey to reigniting the spark into your home, you can send me an email at onome@sparklingmarriageacademy.com.

I provide group and one-on-one coaching services for those who need a personalised touch from me as they work on transforming their marriages into the home they always dreamt of.

Onome Adeyemo

I will not fail to mention that you cannot do all these alone. GOD is the only foundation on which every marriage is built that cannot be shaken.

I will appreciate your feedback and always remember to "Be The Change You Wish To See."

Remember, the email address is onome@sparklingmarriageacademy.com.

Onome Adeyemo

FEEDBACK:

Feel free to share your experiences with me after practising the exercises in this book. I also think it will be a good idea to hang out sometime with other couples especially if you are in Nigeria. We can always work something out.

Please send me your responses to the questions below.

Were the tasks so difficult after all?

Did they feel like a worthwhile adventure?

Please share, share, share! I am very sure some other couples will need to know.

I wish you a blissful marriage even as we ride together in this journey.

About the Author

I am Onome Adeyemo. I am a wife, mother, sister, daughter, a marriage coach and the founder of The Sparkling Marriage Academy (TSMA). I help married couples reignite the spark in their homes. The Sparkling Marriage Academy is the place to be if you need to bring back the early (butterfly in your stomach) days you shared with your spouse.

To know more, join our Facebook community where we constantly dish out awesome contents that will help you and your spouse experience a refreshed life again.

CONNECT WITH ME

You may connect with me via my different social media handles:

EMAIL: onome@sparklingmarriageacademy.com

FACEBOOK GROUP:

www.facebook.com/groups/TheSparklingMarriageAcademy

INSTAGRAM:

www.instagram.com/thesparklingmarriageacademy

SCHEDULE A CALL: bit.ly/marriagespark

TSMA MENTORING HUB: bit.ly/SparkleHub

WEBSITE: www.sparklingmarriageacademy.com

APPENDIX

TSMA – The Sparkle Marriage Academy

TMI – Too much Information

SP&C – Strictly Private & Confidential